LITTLE TIGER PRESS
An imprint of Magi Publications
1 The Coda Centre, 189 Munster Road, London SW6 6AW
www.littletigerpress.com

First published in Great Britain 2005

ISBN 978-1-84506-035-0

A CIP catalogue record for this book is available
from the British Library.

Printed in China

2 4 6 8 10 9 7 5 3

All About Baby

Place baby's picture here

This baby's name is

_____

LITTLE TIGER PRESS
London

The Day I Was Born

The date I was born was: _____

The day was: _____

The place was: _____

The time was: _____

a.m. ☐   p.m. ☐

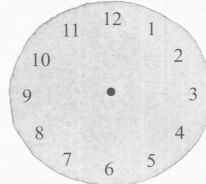

This is what I looked like:

Place picture here

The colour of my hair was: _____

My eyes were: _____

I weighed _____

and I was _____ long.

My Birth

The first signs that I would soon be born were:

_____

_____

_____

The time it took for me to be

born was: _____

These people were present at my birth:

_____

_____

_____

Special things Mummy and Daddy remember about my

birth are: _____

_____

_____

_____

The first people Mummy and Daddy rang were:

_____

_____

Before I Was Born

The date Mummy and Daddy found out they were

expecting me was: _____

The date I was due to be born was: _____

Place the scan here

This is a

picture of me

in Mummy's

tummy.

These are some of the things that Mummy remembers about

being pregnant: _____

_____

_____

Mummy thought I
was going to be a
boy ☐ girl ☐

Daddy thought I
was going to be a
boy ☐ girl ☐

If I was a boy I might have been given these names:

_____

If I was a girl I might have been given these names:

_____

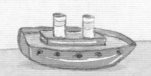

My Family

Mummy's
mummy
_____
_____

Mummy's
daddy
_____
_____

Mummy's
siblings
_____
_____

Mummy
_____
_____

ME
_____
_____

My siblings
_____
_____

Daddy's
daddy

_____

_____

Daddy's
mummy

_____

_____

Daddy

_____

_____

Daddy's siblings

_____

_____

Some other members of my family are:

_____

_____

My First Few Days

My first visitors were: _____

_____

_____

My first gifts were: _____

_____

The first clothes I wore were:

_____

_____

The first time I was given a bath was:

_____

The first time I travelled in a car was:

_____

The first time I went in a buggy was:

_____

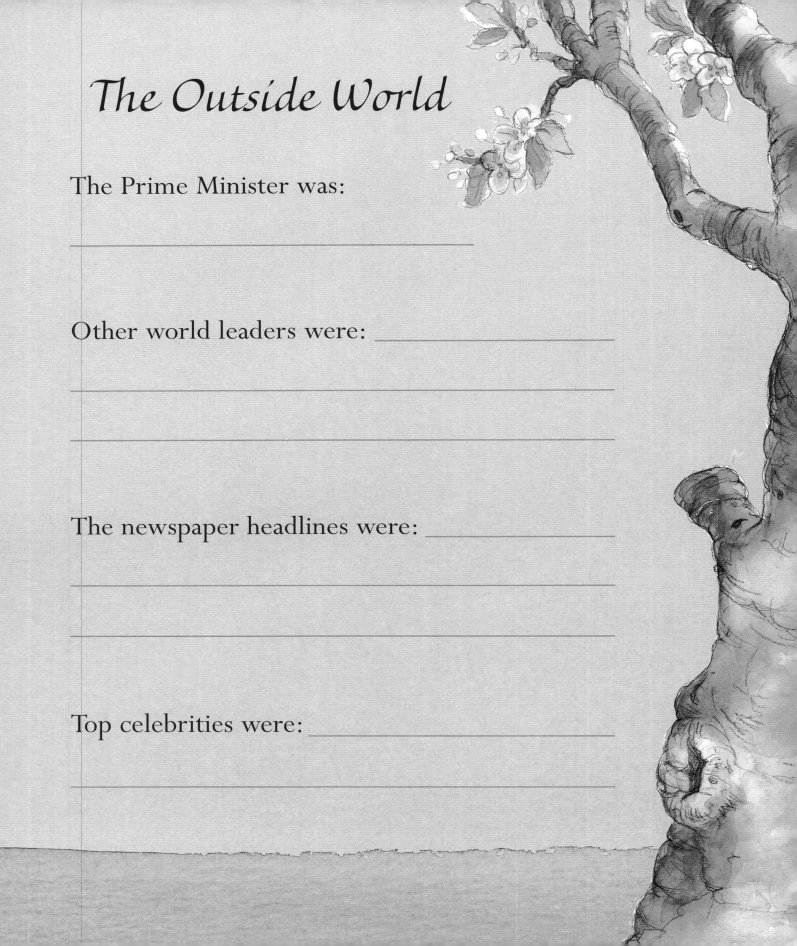

The Outside World

The Prime Minister was:

_____

Other world leaders were: _____

_____

_____

The newspaper headlines were: _____

_____

_____

Top celebrities were: _____

_____

Top songs were:

_____

_____

Top TV programmes were:

_____

_____

Top films were: _____

_____

A first class stamp cost: _____

My Home

The address of my first home was:

_____

_____

The other people who lived in my home were:

_____

_____

The first time I slept there was: _____

_____

The room I slept in was: _____

_____

Regular visitors were:

_____

_____

_____

First Milestones

The first time I slept

through the night was:

_____

The date Mummy and Daddy knew for sure

I could smile was: _____

The date I discovered

my hands was:

_____

The date I first

clapped was:

_____

The date Mummy and Daddy
saw my first tooth was:

_____

I first rolled over when I was

_____ old.

I could sit up by myself
when I was _____ old.
I started to crawl when
I was _____ old.

These are some other important milestones:

_____

_____

_____

Eating

The first solid food I ate was:

_____

_____

I was _____ old.

I first held a cup when I was _____ old.

I first used a spoon by myself when I was _____ old.

At 6 months, my favourite food was:

_____

At 9 months, my favourite food was:

_____

At 12 months, my favourite food was:

_____

Playing

My best friends were:

_____

_____

My favourite soft

toy was called:

_____

Other favourite toys were:

_____

_____

My favourite books were:

_____

_____

My favourite songs were:

_____

_____

Other things I liked to do were:

_____

_____

_____

Special Occasions

My first festival was: _____

I spent it with these people: _____

_____

_____

I went here on holiday: _____

_____

_____

These are some other places

where I stayed: _____

_____

This is a picture of me having fun:

Place picture here

Some other

important events in my

first year were: _____

_____

_____

My First Birthday

People who celebrated my birthday with me were:

_____

_____

Some gifts that I was given were:

_____

_____

My favourite gift was:

_____

For tea we had:

_____

This is what I looked like on my first birthday:

Place picture here

The colour of my hair was: _____

My eyes were: _____

I weighed _____

and I was _____ long.

I changed a lot in one year!